WITH STEINBECK in the SEA of CORTEZ

WITH STEINBECK in the SEA of CORTEZ

By Sparky Enea

as told to Audry Lynch

Cover photograph courtesy of Sparky Enea

This book was printed in the United States of America.

To order additional copies of this book, contact:
Xlibris Corporation
1-888-795-4274
www.Xlibris.com
Orders@Xlibris.com
56261

Contents

ACKNOWLEDGEMENTS

I wish to thank the following: Bruce W. Miller for his editorial expertise; Diane Hangar for precise transcriptions of the interview tapes; Pat Kaspar for her editorial criticism; Jan Stiles for marketing advice; Hal Rausch for legal opinion, Patricia Lynch for public relations, Meera and Steve Lester of The Writer's Connection for ongoing advice and information. I would also like to thank the following: my family for their patience and encouragement about the "other man in my life," Steinbeck: Joseph McKenna, my father, Gregory Lynch, my husband, my children: Stephanie Atchinson, Roberta Lynch and Gregory Lynch, Jr. and my granddaughter, Jenelle Smith. Special thanks to all my friends who have patiently listened to my Steinbeck tales for years.

To all the people in my life who have ever believed in me, my writing, and my interest in John Steinbeck.

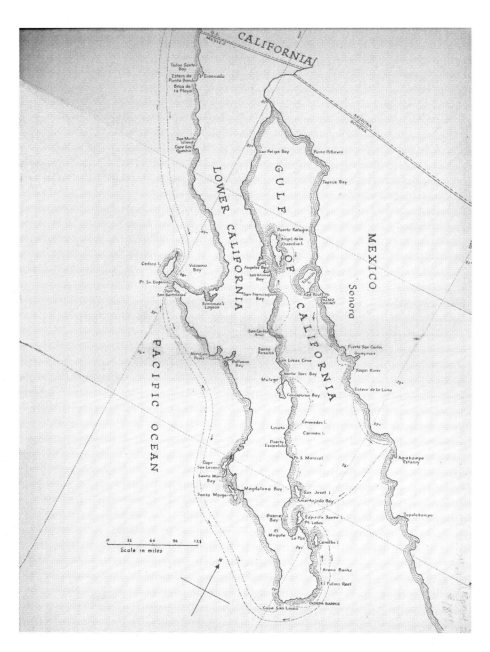

The Sea of Cortez, from Steinbeck's book.

FOREWORD

JOHN STEINBECK was born February 27, 1902, in Salinas, California to an upper middle class family. His father, John Ernst Steinbeck was a businessman and former Treasurer of Monterey County. His mother, formerly Olive Hamilton, had been a teacher in a one-room schoolhouse before her marriage. John had two older sisters, Beth and Esther, and one younger sister, Mary. The family lived in a comfortable Victorian home on Central Avenue—later described in *East of Eden*.

Steinbeck's homelife was enriched by an early exposure to books. A childhood favorite was *Malory's Le Morte d'Arthur* which introduced him to the magic of storytelling. Many years later he would dutifully translate it into modern English. The elder Steinbecks were active in the local Episcopal Church, St. Paul's, so Steinbeck attended services and Sunday school regularly. This early exposure to the Bible instilled in him a lifelong reverence for the printed word.

He attended local schools and graduated from Salinas High School. In most ways he appeared to lead a typical boy's life at the turn of the century. There was a difference, however—and his friends and classmates in later years classified him as a loner. He roamed the countryside, sometimes on his own red pony, storing up impressions of the land that became vivid description in his books.

In the midst of the great Salinas Valley, John Steinbeck grew up restless and preoccupied. He cast about looking for excitement and substance to fill his interior life. He loved listening to local stories and many of them appeared in such works as *The Pastures of Heaven* and *The Long Valley*.

In 1919 he entered Stanford University and embarked on an erratic five year relationship with that school. Although he never graduated, he was awarded many honorary college degrees during his lifetime. The years at Stanford influenced this unconventional student in many ways. His early stories appeared in the *Stanford Spectator*. He also took a writing class from

9

Edith Mirrielees who taught short story writing. During the summer he took marine biology courses at Hopkins Marine Station in Pacific Grove.

After leaving Stanford Steinbeck shared an apartment in North Beach with college classmate Carl Wilhelmson. At 23, Steinbeck dressed and looked the part of a bohemian. He continued writing but in the face of numerous rejections from publishers he sailed for New York City to try his luck. Again he felt defeated but his New York stay led to some interesting experiences: a job on the New York American, a tragic love affair with a Greenwich Village Follies showgirl, and a job as a hod-carrier in the construction of Madison Square Garden.

In New York he showed some of his stories to interested people including a maverick publisher, Robert M. McBride & Company. McBride had the reputation for publishing relatively unknown writers. On one occasion a greatly disappointed Steinbeck made a nuisance of himself and was thrown out of their corporate offices. Ironically, it was McBride who would eventually publish his first novel, *Cup of Gold*.

Discouraged again by rejection, he returned to California to the land and people he loved. In 1930, he married Carol Henning—the first of his three wives. They moved to Pacific Grove to the Steinbeck family's summer cottage where they lived on a monthly stipend of twenty-five dollars from his father and the earnings of Carol's various jobs.

Soon after this move Steinbeck met Edward F. Ricketts, a handsome and remarkable man by all accounts. "Doc" Ricketts collected and sold marine specimens from a Cannery Row laboratory supply house called Pacific Biologicals. He greatly influenced Steinbeck's life and writing. Steinbeck would spend long hours in the lab soaking up atmosphere, talking, drinking beer, and arguing the eternal subjects. Steinbeck paid him his highest honor when he made him a character in several novels.

First, however, Steinbeck wrote the book that would make him famous—*Tortilla Flat*. Hurriedly written, this novel would set Steinbeck's career on end. The sudden fame garnered from *Tortilla Flat* took him by surprise. He much preferred the more serious *In Dubious Battle* which increased his already growing reputation. His next book *Of Mice and Men* sold 100,000 copies within a few weeks of publication.

The Grapes of Wrath, one of his finest novels won the Pulitzer Prize and caused a great deal of controversy when it was issued in 1939. It was from this turmoil that the publicity-shy Steinbeck was hiding when he chartered Captain Tony Berry's boat, the Western Flyer, and embarked on his expedition to the Sea of Cortez. He set off to Baja saying "about the only heroes left are the scientists and the poor" (Benson, 1984: 402).

This sojourn involved seven people: Steinbeck, Carol, his wife, Ricketts, "Tex", the engineer, Captain Berry, Sparky Enea, and "Tiny" Colleto. The trip would provide camaraderie, carefree eating and drinking, and long conversations. The trip to the Sea of Cortez represented a dream and an escape.

Later, Steinbeck, with Ricketts' help, would write *The Sea of Cortez, A Leisurely Journal of Travel and Research* from "Doc's" sea log and Captain Berry's Ship's Log. Steinbeck intended to keep notes but never did. He always looked for new departures in his writing and a book about this trip would combine the elements of fiction and non-fiction, the serious and the romantic. It is a major statement of Steinbeck's philosophy of life including what he learned from Edward F. Ricketts. In the end, the trip turned out so well that the entire crew vowed to do it again some day. No one could foresee that "Doc" would die in an unfortunate accident and none of them would ever travel to the Sea of Cortez again. Shortly thereafter, Steinbeck would leave California for residence in the East. An acrimonious divorce with Carol would ensue. He went on to write more than a half dozen novels, two of which are very fine—*East of Eden* and *Cannery Row*. In 1962, he won the Nobel Prize for Literature.

This book is designed to let you glimpse into that rarefied time. It was a happy, carefree time before the harsh realities of World War II would begin. We see Steinbeck before he became a world traveller, a war correspondent, and a friend and adviser to presidents. Thanks to Sparky's recollections, we can recapture the innocence and freedom of the voyagers. No one knew that it was a special time—one that would never come again.

Audry Lynch 1991

A LIST OF JOHN STEINBECK'S MAJOR WORKS

Cup of Gold 1929
The Pastures of Heaven 1932
To A God Unknown 1933
Tortilla Flat 1935
In Dubious Battle 1936
Of Mice and Men 1937
The Red Pony 1937
The Long Valley 1938
The Grapes of Wrath 1939
The Forgotten Village 1941
Sea of Cortez 1941
The Moon Is Down 1942
Bombs Away 1942
Cannery Row 1945
The Wayward Bus 1947
The Pearl 1947
A Russian Journal 1948
Burning Bright 1950
The Log From the Sea of Cortez 1951
East of Eden 1952
Sweet Thursday 1954
Short Reign of Pippin IV 1957
Once There Was A War 1958
The Winter of Our Discontent 1961
Travels With Charley 1962
American and Americans 1966
Journal of A Novel 1969
The Acts of King Arthur and His Noble Knights 1977

PREPARATIONS

How did I, "Sparky" Enea, a local Sicilian fisherman, become part of John Steinbeck's famous expedition to the Sea of Cortez? Well, first of all, he wasn't very famous when I first met him. Of course I had known him by sight at a lot of the local bars for years. He was a big, crude-looking guy dressed in a seaman's cap, old levis, and a turtle-neck sweater who used to hang out on the wharves looking like a bum.

He came down to the wharf on March 1, 1940, and I've never forgotten it. At the time he was just another guy trying to charter a boat, but I sensed that this was the start of a very special voyage. One week later we were ready to go!

Us local fishermen called Steinbeck a "radical" because he was associated with the famous union organizer, Harry Lloyd Bridges. At that time Bridges was trying to get the Monterey fishermen into the AFL-CIO, but we were afraid of losing our local autonomy. We wanted to be able to elect our own local officials. So we were backing Harry Lundberg and the Seafarer's Union. There were some ugly confrontations and we thought some of them were caused by Steinbeck writing propaganda for Bridges. Later we found out that it was his wife, Carol, who had written the propaganda.

Also, Steinbeck and his friends had helped the pickers against the growers in the lettuce strike of 1937 in Salinas. Some of his artist and writer friends worked for the WPA at that time and their jobs were threatened if they didn't stop agitating the strikers but they kept on anyway. It seemed to us that Steinbeck was a traitor to his class and his family's friends and neighbors, the growers. So Steinbeck wasn't too popular at that time among us fishermen. We just chalked him off as a local "radical." That's probably why, when he first came down to the wharf to hire a boat for the trip to the Sea of Cortez, nobody would listen to him.

On the deck of the Western Flyer, Left to right, Sparky Enea, "Tex" Travis, Tal and Rich Lovejoy, Carol Steinbeck, John Steinbeck and Tiny.

John Steinbeck. Sonya Nostowiak, Courtesy of the Steinbeck Archives, Salinas Public Library. Salinas CA

We knew his friend, "Doc" Ricketts, a lot better. "Doc" was a marine biologist who had a lab on Cannery Row. Mostly we saw both of them at a bar in Monterey called Brucia's Tavern down on Alvarado Street that catered to local fishermen and cannery workers. Steinbeck and Ricketts would come into Brucia's with a group of their friends who were mostly writers and artists. They hung out with a young Bohemian crowd that included Rich Lovejoy, a writer and artist. Later Steinbeck gave his Pulitzer Prize money to further Rich's writing career. Tal, his wife, was the daughter of a Russian priest who came originally from Sitka, Alaska. Elwood and Barbara Graham were both artists and Remo Scardigli was a sculptor and his wife, Virginia, a teacher. Frank Lloyd was an electrician and his wife, Marjorie, was a writer who also later went into real estate. Webster "Toby" Street was a lawyer and he had been a roommate of Steinbeck's at Stanford University. His current wife, Peggy, was a musician and folk-singer. Pol Zerbeck was a sound technician who made record machines for John and "Doc". Bruce Ariss was an artist and his wife, Jean, a novelist. "Doc" was a marine biologist. Another member of the crowd was Jimmy Costello, a reporter for the Monterey Peninsula Herald.

We all went to Brucia's Tavern because Brucia would help anyone in trouble who came to him whether they lived on Cannery Row, in Monterey, or from anywhere else for that matter. He acted as a go-between for the person in trouble with the law. One of the main things he did was to help people with their citizenship papers. In addition to Brucia's Tavern, Steinbeck and his friends also frequented a Spanish-American restaurant alongside the Heritage Harbor called The First Brick House.

After some dockside negotiation my brother-in-law, Captain Berry and Steinbeck settled on a six-week charter for $2500. Captain Berry hired me as a deckhand for $150. That was small wages even for 1940 so you're probably wondering why I agreed to go. For one thing it was a good way to earn a little extra money between fishing seasons. Besides, I had never been to a foreign port so this would be my first one. At the time of the trip Steinbeck had earned a good deal of fame but I didn't think much about it. I knew he was a good writer because I had read *Tortilla Flat*. I knew the guys he was talking about and I still think it's his best book.

We were all surprised to hear that Carol, John's wife, was scheduled to go along with us. Captain Berry set aside one private compartment with two bunks for the Steinbecks, but they never slept together once during the entire trip which also puzzled us. Steinbeck slept with the rest of the crew and Carol stayed by herself. Captain Berry told me that Carol would be the cook for the trip, but she never cooked a meal. But that's another story which I'll get to later.

Next Captain Berry hired Hall Travis whose nickname was "Tex" to be our engineer. He was a tall, lanky guy who was engaged to be married when we got back from our trip. Spencer Tracy was supposed to go with us, but he got tied up on a picture and had to cancel at the last minute. "Toby" (Webster) Street, a local lawyer and Stanford classmate of Steinbeck's, was also scheduled to go, but he got busy so he only went with us as far as San Diego.

When he heard about all our plans my best friend, "Tiny" Coletto, decided that he wanted to go, too. "Tiny" and I were both born in 1910, exactly two months apart. "Tiny" was the older one. My family lived on Calle Principal after 1919, and the Coletto's backyard and ours bordered on each other. Best of all we lived about 300 yards from the old Fisherman's Wharf and the first sardine cannery built on the Row, F.E. Booth. As young boys we learned to swim in the water alongside of Booth's Cannery. There was also a sandy beach there where we would go clamming together.

Tiny (left), Hall Travis (Tex) (middle), Sparky Enea,(right).This photograph was taken just before the trip. Courtesy Tony Berry.

There was a group of neighborhood boys, about 16 of us, from the ages of 10 to 15. Sometimes we got into trouble and we were always fighting among ourselves. "Tiny's" older brother, Sal, bought us some boxing gloves to teach us how to defend ourselves.

Word got around that we had a boxing club and the Elks Lodge asked "Tiny" and me to put on a fight at their Monday night meeting. We put on a good show and in appreciation the members showered us with money—dimes, quarters and even dollar bills. In all we collected about $25 to give to our folks and I was thrilled when my Mother let me keep a dollar.

*The famous match! Tiny, (left) Sparky,
(right) 1921, 11 years old.*

"Tiny" and I attended Monterey Grammar School together but we didn't graduate from Monterey Union High School together. I graduated in 1931 but before that "Tiny" kept a girl out all night. His family was afraid she might be pregnant so they made him join the Navy for four years. Women were always crazy about "Tiny."

In the old neighborhood there were mostly fishing families: Lucido, DiMaggio, Dutra, Ferrante and Russo. We all had good times together. After "Tiny" got out of the Navy we resumed our friendship. After all we had spent years sharing everything together—school, boxing, getting in trouble and even girls.

Naturally when he heard about the trip to the Sea of Cortez, he wanted to go, too. He asked Steinbeck for a job on the trip but John said he couldn't afford to hire him. Finally, they both agreed that "Tiny" could come along, without pay, and just work off his room and board. Captain Berry was glad because now that meant we could have three wheel watches; three hours on and six hours off.

Tiny, (left), Sparky, (right). La Paz, 1940. Courtesy Captain Tony Berry.

"Tiny" was about my size, but maybe an inch taller than 5'1". He was 30, about 118 pounds, and had just gotten out of the Navy. While he was in the Navy, he had won the bantamweight boxing championship at Long Beach. By the way, we later found out that the girl never had become pregnant.

Let me put it this way."Tiny" was a real ladies' man. At this time he was going around with a woman called Dawn, one of Flora Woods' girls. "Tiny" had a shiny, sporty black Hudson Roadster with a rumbleseat so when he decided to go on the trip with us, he left the car with Dawn to take care of and that's why she met us in San Diego on the return trip. "Doc" Ricketts was the other member of the crew. As Steinbeck's best friend and a marine biologist, basically he was the reason behind the whole trip. Since he wanted to collect specimens for the lab, but didn't have the money, Steinbeck was paying for the whole trip. In contrast to Steinbeck, "Doc" was absolutely immaculate. He was much shorter than Steinbeck, but well-built. In those days "Doc" wore a small Van Dyke beard which was always neatly trimmed. Most people thought he was a very distinguished-looking guy.

At first Steinbeck wanted to leave on Sunday, March 10, but we said, "No, it has to be Monday" because we didn't want to miss the big fishermen's Sardine Fiesta on Sunday. We asked John to come to it, but he never made it. I was surprised that he wrote about it. Anyway in *The Log From the Sea of Cortez* he got some of the facts wrong. I guess sometimes he was still writing fiction.

I'll never forget that particular fiesta. It cost thirty-seven thousand dollars and we hired every waitress in town. There were all kinds of parties before and after the fiesta. There must have been about eighty-four purse seiners between seventy-five and eighty feet long lined up along the Monterey Wharf. Most of them were decorated with flowers and flags. The smell of good food was everywhere and friends and relatives were getting on board the boats. One of the best parts of the fiesta was the street dance. It was the biggest and best fiesta we ever had. In fact we never had another one after that.

Of course the food was great, but mainly everyone looked forward to the contests: the skiff race, the greased pole walk, and the waterbarrel tilt. Of all of these, the greased pole walk caused the most excitement. The pole was raised forty feet over the water. Then it was smeared first with a gallon of lard and next with a gallon of axle grease. The rule was; you could not fall on the pole and muscle your way to the flag. You just had to maintain your balance, walk out and get the flag, and have the flag in your hand when you hit the water.

The fleet at fiesta time. Courtesy of the Enea family.

Most of the guys moved too fast or too soon. An old Sicilian fisherman, Bautista DiMaggio, took me aside and gave me good advice. He knew about it because he had participated in contests like this in the Old Country. He told me, "You've got good balance, "Sparky" so just walk slowly. Don't try to run." It worked! I won the contest in two different fiestas. That contest was one of my best and I landed in the water holding the flag high to win the first prize of twenty-five dollars.

In preparation for the trip Captain Berry told me to order the ship stores so I ordered the best brands of everything, Del Monte for the canned goods. There were: boxes of spaghetti, cases of peaches, tomatoes, pineapples, Romano cheeses, canned milk, flour and cornmeal, gallons of olive oil, tomato paste, crackers, butter and jam, catsup and rice, beans and bacon, and canned meats and vegetables. I didn't bring along any recipes—only the ones I knew in my head from my parents—because I thought Carol would do all the cooking.

Then came the booze. In those days, before you left Immigration, you could buy all the liquor you wanted. I bought three or four cases of Canadian Club, V.O. and I.W. Harper. I also bought several cartons of Camel cigarettes for all of us except Captain Berry who smoked Lucky Strikes. Steinbeck usually rolled his own with Bull Durham tobacco or smoked Wings. Wine was called for so I had plenty of that and a few cases of beer. Mainly the crew was looking forward to Mexican beer, especially Carta Blanca. John and "Doc" brought an old ice chest with a one-watt battery on top to keep the beer cold. That just made me laugh because I knew it would never work. We kept the ice in a big Coca Cola box to keep things cold. That's why we only took along a few days supply of meat. We figured that we could get our really big order in San Diego.

Just before we took off we had a big party on board the boat. The Western Flyer was only about two years old then, 77 feet long, and it really looked good. Wives, friends, and girl friends came down to see us off. There must have been at least twenty or thirty people. One of the photographers came down from the Monterey Peninsula Herald to take our picture. When the picture was developed, I noticed that Steinbeck was hiding his face behind Carol's head. He never wanted his picture taken. I guess it was because of all his political activities. In fact John told the crew he didn't want any of us to take his picture during the trip. Once I sneaked a couple of shots of him and Captain Berry up on the deck. The sculptor used that photo to model the bust of him on Cannery Row

Well, as it turns out, I was a fisherman for over fifty years. During that time I remember lots of fishing trips. As we left Monterey harbor that day I felt happy and excited, but I had no way of knowing that this Steinbeck /Ricketts expedition to the Sea of Cortez would be the trip that I would remember the most of all!

BULL SESSIONS AND TALES OF CANNERY ROW

At night on the *Western Flyer* we would read or sit around, drink beer and talk. On the way to San Diego we had a long discussion about the Old Man of the Sea. There are many stories that old fishermen tell about this creature and Steinbeck, in particular, seemed fascinated by them. Basically, however, we know it's just a sea elephant.

There are big colonies of sea elephants around Ana Nuevo. Some of the bulls are about thirty or forty feet long. From a distance they resemble all sorts of things and the fishermen sometimes imagine they are monsters, someone smoking a pipe, a sea monster with two jaws, and other times they imagine it's a creature with long, black hair. After all the stories and sightings it always turns out to be just another sea elephant.

"Tiny" and I also told Steinbeck stories about the Old Cannery Row. He asked us a lot of questions and we thought he would use them as material for his books. We really felt important.

The real start of Cannery Row came with the Chinese. Their first village, China Point, is now the Hopkins Marine Station of Stanford University. After 1906 they moved to Machbee Beach which is in the center of Cannery Row. When I was a youngster it was just a dirt road with a pump in the middle where they got fresh water. They kept ducks, chickens and pigs. They would fish for abalone and squid and other fish. They had poles with wire baskets in which they dried the fish. There was no refrigeration then so everything was dried. Boy, what a smell!

Gambling was a big part of life in the Chinese section. High Q, Fan Tan and Chinese dominoes were the main games. The gambling dens were very lively and there was some opium smoking, too. One of the biggest gambling dens was located at Franklin and Tyler streets where the Bank of America is now headquartered. A fire finally wiped out the whole village.

Sometimes the Chinese were smuggled in on the fishing boats. Around 1916 my own father and uncle accidentally got involved in it. My Dad kept looking at two old sacks lying up on the deck. He said to my uncle, "I think I saw those sacks move." It kept happening so finally he looked inside and saw that there were two Chinamen in each one of them. He just closed them up and never said another word. At the end of the trip they received a $5 gold piece for each one but he said, "Never again" because it was illegal and he didn't want to take a chance on getting caught.

After the Chinese, the Portuguese whalers came, followed by the Japanese abalone divers. By 1906 the Italian fishermen started to come into the area to fish for salmon and sardines. My uncle and father came originally from Isla de Fenmi, by way of Pittsburgh, California. Monterey Bay was full of sardines in those days and F.E. Booth told my father and uncles, "Why don't you fish for sardines and we'll try to can them." They started with four or five boats, with a five to six ton limit, and Booth opened the first cannery. The men would stay for the season, go back to Italy, get their wives pregnant, and come back for fishing until gradually they started to bring the wives and families over.

After World War I, the boats got bigger and were called lampara boats and my father built one. A lampara boat is thirty-two feet long and can hold twenty, thirty, forty or over one hundred tons of fish. Six men sit on each side to pull the giant fish nets called "wings", two hundred feet long, to catch a sardine haul.

Then Hovden built his cannery. More boats appeared and more fishermen were hired and finally someone built a reduction plant to make fish meal and fish oil. Sometimes the plant made fertilizer or paints from the fish remains. It took tons of fish for these purposes and at one time there were several reduction plants on the Row.

In 1927 a still bigger boat than the lampara appeared and they were called purse seiners. They could carry between seventy-five to one hundred and fifty tons of sardines in their fish hold. They ranged between seventy-six to eighty feet in length. Before them everything was done by hand. The purse seiners modernized everything because the net was pulled in by boom and tackle.

Western Flyer low in water getting ready to unload 120 tons of sardines. Photo taken in Monterey before the trip.
Courtesy the Enea family.

Other canneries came in after Hovden—E.B. Gross, Carmel, Sea Pride, Cal Pack, San Xavier, Monterey Canning Company and Del Mar. My father opened his own cannery after World War II but it was too late. The sardines started to disappear and no one expected or could have predicted that. He lost his cannery and all our money. My future wife, Mary Correa, was a cannery worker and called the "fastest fish-cutter on the Row" in her day. She started working in the canneries when she was only twelve years old. Over the years she worked in most of the canneries along the Row. In all, she worked for fifty years as a fish cutter.

In addition to the cannery workers, the madams and the prostitutes were just part of Monterey life. Everyone went to the houses—doctors, judges, politicians. You could go to the houses just to drink and dance too, without visiting the prostitutes. Several "respectable" people went there just for the drinking and dancing. In fact I remember when my cousin, Buck Russo, became a Councilman and then Mayor of Monterey in 1937 or 1938. He held his victory party in one of the bordellos and everyone came there to celebrate.

When we left Monterey we knew all our friends were curious about the Mexican prostitutes and if they were different from the ones in Monterey. They wanted "Tiny" and me to find out. We knew we'd be asked a million questions when we got back.

We told Steinbeck all the stories we knew about fishermen, cannery workers and prostitutes because we thought we were giving him information for his books. Steinbeck and Ricketts liked the fishermen and cannery stories, but mainly they liked to talk about women. "Tiny" and I were well acquainted with the houses on the Row so they liked our stories about them. In our eyes Steinbeck and Ricketts were always a couple of "studs."

There were three whorehouses on the Row at that time—the Marine Apartments, Flora Woods and La Ida's. Sometimes even legitimate women went into them because they had jukeboxes and bars. They were places to drink and dance after hours. The soldiers from the Presidio used to go there and it was the military who finally had them closed down after World War II. The madams had the girls checked by their doctors once a week and the army doctors checked them weekly, too, so we knew they were always clean.

Steinbeck and Ricketts were always interested in stories about women. They kept egging us on to tell our whorehouse stories. "Doc," on the other hand, was a real friend of Flora Woods, the main Monterey madam. She would send him over cold beer to the lab after hours if his supply ran out and he did a lot of favors for her with the girls. My cousin told me about Flora's history. In the 1800's, all the whalers came from Boston and Gloucester before they moved to California. Flora came from one of those families. Evidently she didn't like that life and so she got into the rackets. We knew that she had been born at Point Lobos and had been a mid-wife in her early years. When I knew her in the thirties she was a big, fat woman around two hundred pounds.

I knew her daughter, Lorraine, even better because she was in my class in high school. Lorraine was fat and looked a lot like her mother and was a real lonesome kid. No one would dance with her at school dances so I did. All the fishermen used to dance at the Roseland Ballroom on Friday and Saturday nights so I used to dance with Lorraine there, too. Later she died of cancer in her early thirties.

Lorraine's mother, Flora, was a remarkable businesswoman. On Thanksgiving and Christmas Day, Flora was a one-woman charity organization. She got lists of all the poor families in town from all the churches. She had her own fleet of taxis to deliver packages of food to poor people all over town. Every year she did that and no one ever mentioned her name as the person who made all the donations.

Flora's girls were clean and good-looking. There wasn't any financial competition among the three "houses": Flora's, La Ida's, and the Marine Apartments. At first they all charged a dollar fifty and then they went to two dollars and finally three. They all charged the same rates. When Flora got a new girl, our police chief got first crack at her and would drive her around town so everyone could see how she looked.

When I was about eighteen or nineteen I made my first visit to the Lone Star. The Lone Star had a big, long bar. Originally they served food there, too. There was a dance hall and about ten rooms upstairs. There was a beaded curtain that separated the entry hall from the bar and restaurant. As a rule Flora would sit there all night and then sleep in the daytime. We went in and said, "Hello," and Flora looked at me and said, "Hey, Enea come over here." When I did she asked, "What are you doing here?" "I'm gonna take on one of your girls", I replied. "You're not old enough," she answered "Hell, I'm 22," I says. "Don't tell me how old you are," she shot back. "I changed your diapers when you were a baby." I was surprised by that, but she finally let me in. After that she never bothered me. She would even take you "on the cuff" and I owed her $3 when I went into the service.

I asked my oldest brother about it and he said, "She lived near us in the old days. She was a midwife." He told me she had lived in a two-storey house alongside my uncle's house. It was called "The Greenhouse" and she had two girls working for her. All my relatives lived within a two hundred yard area. In those days there were no doctors so most of us were delivered by midwives.

Flora Woods. Steinbeck Archives. Salinas Public Library.

I got to goin' great with one of Flora's girls and she asked me to take her to the Lettuce Inn in Salinas. She loved to dance and she paid all the bills. One night I met "Tiny" there with another one of the girls.

My brother loaned me his car and, if you had a car, the girls were always anxious to get out of town. If it was awful hot, they would go swimming with us in the Carmel River which was really primitive in those days. There was a swimming hole called Schultze's Ranch that had a road right to the river. We'd swim and bathe in the sunshine and sometimes bring a steak and barbecue it. We never drank, though, because the girls had to go back to work at night.

Sometimes they would tell us about all the "weirdos" that they ran into at work. One man, who owned a nightclub, used to bring his wife and make his wife watch him while he took on a girl. Another one wanted a girl to cuss his mother out, calling her a son of a bitch. Some of them wanted to be spanked. A few rich lesbians from Pebble Beach used to send taxis over for some of the girls to come directly to their houses.

So these are the kinds of stories we told Steinbeck about. At night we would drink and have these bull sessions. Later on when we read his books, "Tiny" and I were disappointed because he left out so much good material.

Drinking and telling stories at night was a good way to pass the time while we waited for our wheel watches. The wheel watches were six hours long. "Tiny" and I were partners, Steinbeck and "Tex", Captain Berry and Ricketts. Steinbeck made a big deal about us getting off course when "Tiny" and I had the wheel watch but that only happened once on a night when there was a big mirage. It made it difficult for us to judge distance.

In San Diego "Toby" Street left us to get back to work. We were surprised to see a lot of Japanese shrimp boats. Of course it was 1940, but we didn't realize at that time that a big war was about to break out. In 1940 San Diego was a small, growing city along the waterfront. There were about four hundred or five hundred beautiful yachts docked in the marinas. There were no big hotels or motels and the parks were lovely.

Carol told me to buy fresh meat so I did. I bought: two orders of steak, two orders of roast beef, two orders of hamburg, two orders of stew meat and extra lunch meat as well as fresh bread. We didn't have any refrigeration in those days, only three hundred pounds of ice. When Carol saw what I bought she said, "Turn half of that back. We're going to eat fish on the way." The grocery man said, "Don't worry about it" and he took half of it back.

I was still expecting Carol to be the cook, but she went to bed. Captain Berry said, "Why don't you cook up some chicken for supper?" so I did. The next morning we put out fishing lines and I caught five or six bonita. I cleaned them up and asked her, "What do you want to do with them?" And she said, "Well, do you mind cooking again? I've got a hangover."

Carol was supposed to be the cook for the trip but I had cooked every meal since we started. I was getting used to making the breakfast every day. On Thursdays and Sundays I was in the routine of making spaghetti. I had brought along ten pounds of flour and some yeast for her to make fresh bread but they were unopened. Luckily I had brought along two dozen boxes of biscuit powder so I kept making biscuits. She kept saying, "I'm going to make chicken cacciatore for everyone" but nothing was happening. Every night around six Captain Berry would ask me if Carol had started cooking yet. When I said, "No" he would reply, "Well, you better get started then." On the trip Carol finally did cook one thing—a lemon meringue pie. It was delicious and everyone gave her compliments, but that's the first and last time she cooked on the entire trip. Slowly but surely I started to realize that I was going to be the one and only cook on the trip to the Sea of Cortez.

COOKING AND PAISANOS

As soon as we got below the Mexican border we were amazed at the color of the water. We had been on lots of fishing trips to different places, but this water was the most beautiful blue we had ever seen. Our first view of Mexico showed a lovely, uncluttered shoreline, clear sunny weather and water ranging between 82 and 90 degrees. There were no hotels or motels and everything looked very primitive. When we were off Point Baja we knew we were in the region of the sea turtle and flying fish, so we put out our fishing lines. Since "Tiny" and I were fishermen, we kept our lines out for the rest of the trip.

Not only was the sea a different color, but we were also seeing different kinds of fish. I caught a skipjack and nobody knew what it was. When I filleted it and cooked it up, everyone enjoyed it.

After we passed Point Lazaro, we caught two small dolphin fish. They cooked up like filet of sole. When we rolled them over on the deck we suddenly saw all kinds of colors—reds, blues, greens. They looked like a rainbow on the deck. They weren't like the porpoises we used to catch in the tuna nets. We had never seen fish like that before!

Steinbeck was right when he said we didn't want to catch porpoises. Once we caught one in a net and it cried so that someone said, "Sounds like a baby around here." It finally broke out of the net and got away. Personally, after hearing them cry like that I could never keep one.

All of us fishermen, even the oldtimers, always respected porpoises. They say that if you get into trouble on the sea, the porpoises will always bring you back to land. There have been a lot of cases where they swim alongside a swimmer until he makes it back to land. That's what they say, so you've got to go along with it.

We were in Magdalena Bay, heading for Cabo San Lucas, when we caught something that didn't turn out to be a success at all. It was a turtle about three feet long. I caught it in a dip net and promised that I would make turtle soup for everyone.

First of all, we didn't even know how to kill it. We got out the axe, but it kept moving even after we cut off the head. Finally we beat it to death. Then we found out we didn't even know how to shell it. When I got the meat out and cooked it, everything turned black. It smelled awful, too, so we wound up throwing the whole mess out. Luckily only Captain Berry and "Tex" and I were there to see this horrible event because the others were out collecting. It was my only cooking disaster throughout the entire trip!

Later, when we got to Guaymas, I found out what to do with a turtle. My brother-in-law, Captain Tony Berry, who is Yugoslavian, ran into another Yugoslavian who said, "This afternoon we're going to have a big turtle dinner at one of the bars. All the big shots go down there after twelve o'clock. Would you fellows be interested in eating it?" "Sure" we said. Then we told him about our turtle experience.

The gardens at this bar were beautiful. It was a big outdoor garden restaurant. There were flowering plants and trees all over the patio. In the middle was a big barbecue pit. It attracted the business crowd and all the big shots from the Japanese shrimp boats.

And they had a big turtle! It must have been, oh my God, one hundred pounds or more. They had sliced it and were barbecuing the meat in the fireplace. After it was cooked they cut it up and put it into the shell again. On the top they put lettuce, tomatos, onions and hot peppers—just like a big tossed salad. It was out of this world.

Then when I told them about my turtle disaster they said, "That's what happens." Then they explained that the turtle is like a pig. You've got to bleed it first. The softest meat is carved out from underneath the shell. When it's done properly, the meat is white and tastes like veal. "Tiny" and I had never seen a turtle like that before in our lives.

If the turtle was a disaster, I have to admit that my spaghetti dinners were always a success. It's a tradition among Sicilians to have spaghetti on Sundays and Thursdays, so I always did that as a ritual on board the Western Flyer. Steinbeck liked it so much that he always bragged about my spaghetti to his friends.

Every time someone came on the wheel watch I always had a pot of fresh coffee waiting for them. There were three shifts and we had fresh coffee ready always for the next shift. I always made big breakfasts for everyone every morning—pancakes, ham and eggs, whatever they wanted. At night I kept expecting Carol to cook the meal, but nothing was happening. When I asked Captain Berry he would just say, "If she doesn't do it, just do it." Looking back on it, maybe she had heard I was a good cook from Peter Ferrante, who knew my family and was a law partner of "Toby" Street.

I learned to cook in 1925 when I was fishing for albacore tuna with my father in Southern California. We'd be travelling five or six boats together.

There were charcoal stoves kept in the hold in those days and they were very efficient. At night we'd be in San Clemente or Catalina and we'd all tie up and cook something.

Once in San Diego the men decided to have a big barbecue. I love to swim, so I went to Mission Beach which had just opened up. Afterwards we went to a burlesque show in town. Then I said, "Geez, that potato soup my Dad made tasted so good, I think I'll make it." So I got a pot, lit the charcoal stove, and put in potatoes, onions and celery. I'd put salt in and then I'd taste it and put more water in. Finally I had to throw it overboard. I told my Dad about it and he said, "What'd you do?" After that I watched him and my older brother cook. Later when he built his boat in '35, we had an old cook, a cousin of Dad's, and he didn't like cooking. So I took over and sometimes I'd ask mother how to cook this and that. That's how I became the cook on my Dad's boat.

As we entered the Sea of Cortez, Captain Berry would get out his copy of the Coast Pilot. Steinbeck was worried about the storms in the area, but luckily we didn't run into one until we were on our way home. Captain Berry also studied the tides, especially the low ones, because that was going to be important for the collecting of the specimens.

Steinbeck brought some books along so we spent some of our time reading. I remember he brought a copy of *The Grapes of Wrath* and we read that. I thought then—and I still do now—that there was a lot of truth in the book. He wrote what he saw. "Tiny" and I also read *Studs Lonigan*. I remember "Tiny" saying at the end of it, "Hey, that's just like me."

Sometimes we'd talk about the Paisanos that Steinbeck wrote about in *Tortilla Flat*. Paisano is a term that means 'pal' or 'buddy' and it can mean many nationalities—Italian, Spanish Mexican or Portuguese. These guys were basically handymen—men like Pilon, Eddie, Andrew Escobar. They would chop wood, fix up your yard or do any other little chores around the house. They didn't want money—just food, mainly wine, and Bull Durham tobacco. When they got drunk, they would fight and cut each other up. John used them for the models of his characters in the book. Andrew Escobar should have been the main character, but I guess John picked out Pilon because he was cockeyed.

The Paisanos all lived in the same neighborhood—the Escobars, Castros, Dutras, Rileys and the Gonzalezes. There was a little valley called Happy Valley and they all lived there. They lived underneath the oak trees because that's where they could get the water from a nearby lake. I argued for years with Jimmy Costello who said Tortilla Flat was above the American Legion Hall which is now Deer Flats.

The guy that Steinbeck called the Pirate was a guy we called Bear Tracks when we were kids of about eight or nine. He always wore a long overcoat, was stooped, carried a cane, and had loads of dogs following him. These were all the strays that he had adopted. We called him names and he would chase us but he could never catch us. The dogs came after us, too, but we ran like hell.

Some of the Paisanos were hard workers. They would go to different homes and chop wood or work in the yards and they did a very good job until they started drinking. Now, if you didn't have a rake or a hoe, or a shovel, they would steal it from one person and go to work for another.

Sometimes they would work for my family, but they never wanted much to eat. They always wanted wine. And if you gave 'em too much wine, then they would get drunk and they wouldn't work. My father would tell my mother, "Put half water and half wine in the pitcher or these guys won't work much." She'd give them about a quart. And at times they got roaring drunk. They were good workers until they got drunk. Then they wouldn't do nothing. She finally got smart. After they got through work she would always give 'em a piece of bread and whatever we had left over, fish or a piece of meat.

A woman across the street from my mother was a bootlegger. She would hide the bottles in her apron and come across the street and hide about a dozen pints of whiskey in my mother's artichoke plants. I went down to check and we'd steal one every once in awhile. One time we urinated a little into it, to get it the same color as the whiskey, and sold it to the Paisanos for twenty-five cents.

This friend of Carol's claimed that Steinbeck stole all these stories about Tortilla Flat from Susan Gregory. Steinbeck and I talked about this because Susan Gregory was my Spanish teacher at Monterey High School. She was gray haired when I knew her and she spoke very good Spanish. She came from an old Mexican-Spanish family, and lived on John Street above the high school.

She knew all these stories and had started to write them down until John came along. She figured he could do it better, so she told him all the stories and whom to interview. There were lots of old time gas station owners that she told him about, like John Napoli or Jack Balboa who could give him lots of information about the characters' many escapades and about their backgrounds. He didn't steal the stuff from her. In fact he dedicated the book to her. So that's what we talked about at night during our bull sessions. As we were getting near the islands near La Paz, Ricketts, Steinbeck and Carol were getting anxious to start collecting the specimens. They kept pouring over the tide books. At first "Tiny" and I weren't interested in that part of the trip. All I knew was that it felt like we had signed on for a six-week party. And it was!

CAPE SAN LUCAS

As we approached Cape San Lucas, we knew we were there as the Two Friars loomed ahead. These are two huge rock formations that did look, at least from a distance, like two giant brothers in brown. They were the landmark we had been waiting for. It had been ninety hours since we had left San Diego and we yearned for land. The Two Friars were a welcome sight for the crew of the Western Flyer.

When we first landed at Cape San Lucas there was a tuna cannery there with a Mexican manager named Frank. He was a graduate of U.C.L.A. When we came in there at two o'clock in the morning, there was supposed to be a wharf and a light there. Well, the wind was blowing and there was a tree there. Sometimes you'd see it and sometimes you wouldn't see it. So we threw the lead line over to make sure we weren't too close to the shore. In the morning we thought we were about a hundred yards offshore. We were actually about half a mile offshore. That's how a mirage fools you.

We washed and shaved the next morning, but we knew we couldn't go ashore until we were cleared by the Mexican officials. Of course we weren't really worried because we knew that Steinbeck had sent for and received our Mexican permits. We also had our passports. It was noon before they rowed out to us and then we were surprised to see that they were wearing 45's in their holsters.

Captain Berry told me to get the galley ready for them. I had made fresh coffee laced with whiskey for the officials. They were friendly and crazy about American cigarettes so we gave them some. We had bought five cases of Camels at fifty cents a carton. In a way we were a little afraid of these guys. They were dark, wore hats and since they were packing 45's, they looked like gangsters.

After they left, we decided to go into town. We were going to use the Hansen Sea Cow, but we couldn't get it to work. It was a little rowboat with an outboard motor. We also had a big skiff about twenty feet long that we used for fishing. This was just the beginning of our troubles with the Sea Cow.

"Tex", our engineer, worked on it all the time. He had been the first engineer hired for the Western Flyer when Tony had the boat built two years ago in Tacoma, Washington. It worked a few times during the trip after "Tex" took it apart and worked on it. He kept working on it so much that it really became his special "project" during the entire trip. Despite all his efforts it seemed like when we wanted it to work and needed it, it just quit on us. Originally Steinbeck had called the little rowboat the Sea Horse, but since it almost never worked, "Tex" had renamed it the Sea Cow. I don't think it had more than a couple of horsepower. In fact, the brother of the Mayor of Pacific Grove, Williams, had sold it to Steinbeck. John didn't know a thing about boats and I don't think it ever worked right.

Steinbeck borrowed somebody's twenty millimeter movie camera. Everywhere we stopped he took pictures of the scenery and the local people. He ought to be ashamed of himself. He didn't know how to run it. After the trip, the fishermen's union was running a smoker of some kind. I asked John if I could borrow the movie. Figured I'd show them a lot of the beautiful scenes we had visited. It's so beautiful down there. I was totally disappointed. Not one picture came out so I had nothing to show them.

At least when the Hansen Sea Cow broke down, we had the skiff on board that doubled as a lifeboat. We called it the Baby Flyer.

When the Sea Cow stalled, we all climbed into the Baby Flyer to head for the town of Cape San Lucas. We found that it was a small, poor town. When we first went to Mexico, it was very primitive.

The Baby Flyer at Porno Reef. Steinbeck and Sparky (on rudder)
in the stern, Carol in middle and Tex in the prow.
Photo, Courtesy of Sparky Enea.

There were lots of nicely outfitted yachts in the harbor. Nowadays they would sell for between two hundred thousand or three hundred thousand dollars. The owners had beautiful clothes on, enjoyed their cocktail parties on the deck and went from place to place fishing because Cape San Lucas is famous for that. They fish for sailfish, swordfish, red rooster or tuna. The other thing that I'll never forget are the beautiful sunrises and sunsets in that place—all blue and pink.

When we got to town "Tiny" and I went shopping for caps because I had lost my seaman's cap in Monterey. In San Diego we bought big straw hats. Now we bought some Panama hats, then headed for a local cantina which was filled with young Mexican guys.

We drank Carta Blanca beer and Steinbeck made an amazing purchase. He bought a bottle of Damiana. It was supposed to be a sex drink. We were going to keep it, take it to Doc's lab when we got back, have a party and see how it affected us. Carol knew about it, too, and we all talked about it a lot on the trip.

After our trip to town, we knew that John, Carol and "Doc" were dying to start their collecting. This was the whole purpose of the trip! They got out their nets and bottles and tubes and put on big rubber boots. Actually they found out that the water was so warm they didn't need them.

Ricketts wanted to see all the different specimens of fish everywhere we stopped. They set a goal of working four or five hours at a stretch. Then the three of them would be back on the deck putting everything in vials and jars and Ricketts would be labelling them and writing loads of notes. Ricketts couldn't believe the wide variety of specimens. It was a lot more than he had expected to find.

"Doc" told "Tiny", "Well, if we sell all these specimens to colleges and high schools, we'll make between $18,000 and $25,000." Captain Berry said, "What? How come you didn't tell me this before? We're bringing back valuable cargo." He thought they should pay him more but that's all that was said. A charter like that nowadays would cost $100,000.

We didn't have much trouble with the tides during our collecting because we had good weather all the way until the return trip. Captain Berry would vplan it all out before we got to each place. That's why sometimes we traveled only two or three hours, sometimes only one, at a time.

"Tiny" and I also wondered if something was going on between Carol and "Doc". Sometimes we'd see Carol and "Doc" talking and giggling together on deck like a couple of teenagers. There was a little window in the boat's galley and Steinbeck would stand there peeking out at the two of them. That happened quite a few times on the trip. Carol and John acted as if there was nothing unusual in their sleeping arrangements. By day they acted like any ordinary couple.

"Tiny" and I didn't go out collecting with them that first day at Cape San Lucas. But there wasn't much to do all day on the boat and we got bored. The next day when they headed for Pulmo Reef, the only coral reef we would see on the trip, "Tiny" and I decided, "Well, let's go with them. It's hot and the water is warm." After that we always helped them with the collecting of the specimens and they liked that.

Of course when we collected, there was a difference. They would use all these scientific names and we wouldn't know what the hell they were talkin' about. We made up our own names for things. For example, once "Tiny" picked up a fish that was spongy-like and looked like a billyclub. He says, "What is this?" Carol mentioned some scientific name and "Tiny" says, "It reminds me of something else." In the book we looked it up and there were two pictures of it. By God, it did resemble something familiar!

Once we saw a little lagoon so we got the rakes and shovels and we went up to the beach to dig up some clams but we couldn't find any. Then we saw these big, yellow and black lightfoot crabs. You try to catch one of them and you'd go this way and they'd go that way. They drove "Tiny" crazy. He went after them with a shovel because he wanted to catch them alive. We even threw rocks at them. He finally fell and hurt his arm right below the elbow. He wound up lying on the sand after a failed attempt to get a crab.

While he was trying to catch the Sally Lightfoot crabs, I started wading around in nice, white water. Every now and then I'd notice something green like seaweed on the bottom. I put my hand down and caught a big, white clam. So I says, "Hey, "Tiny", look. See these little green spots? There's a clam down there." Then I grabbed another one. Wow, did I jump! It was a species of sea urchin. When you grabbed those spines, it was like the sting of a bee for a few seconds. So between sea urchins and Sally Lightfoot crabs, we were pretty careful from then on. In all we picked about a washtub full of white clams.

Back on the boat we were still taking our wheel watches every three hours. Sometimes we'd have to call Captain Tony Berry because he was our navigator in case there was fog or another problem. I was still cooking and everyone took turns doing dishes. "Tex" skipped a few times and, like Steinbeck said, we put a few dirty dishes in his bed to teach him a lesson. One night after we had finished collecting, we ate and drank until about 11 p.m. and then we went to bed. "Tiny" and Carol stayed up and they got into an argument. "Tiny" had been fed up with Carol not doing any of the cooking. Anytime we'd complain, Captain Tony Berry would say, "Just keep cooking, Sparky, until she comes around or else we won't eat."

I was asleep and I don't know what time it was when "Tiny" came in and woke me up. I got up out of the bunk and straightened my clothes. He's grinning and he says, "Come on. Get up." I said, What's the matter?" "Come on over and tell her off."

So I got up and here is Carol crying in the galley. She says to me, "Is it true, "Sparky", that I'm a no-good cheapskate?" I said, "Yeah", and "Tiny" says, "Well, tell her off. She was supposed to be the cook on this trip and she hasn't cooked anything yet. She didn't cook the Chicken Cacciatore like she promised and sent back half the fresh meat."

"Tiny, you can't talk to her like that", I pleaded, but he answered, "Don't tell me I can't say this. I'm not even getting paid as a deckhand. I'm just working for my meals."

He was talking pretty loud and woke up John. Steinbeck came around from the back door and he says, "Hey, the crew is sleeping. What are you guys doing here?"

Carol looked at John and swore at him. He didn't say anything except that he looked at Carol for a minute.

So I said, "Hey, let's break it up. Tiny, don't you ever talk that way again." No one ever mentioned that incident or Carol's cooking for the rest of the trip.

ESPIRITU SANCTO ISLAND

The next day after Pulmo Reef the Western Flyer headed toward a small island called Espiritu Sancto. It would be our last stop before La Paz. "Tiny" and I were looking forward to La Paz because it would have some big city excitement—the kind we had promised our friends back home that we would check out for them.

By the time we got to Espiritu Sancto Island, "Tex" also decided to join us in the collecting. He was a big guy who came along on our trip to pass the time before his wedding. Steinbeck claimed that we put him on a diet for his wedding, but that was pure bull. When I finally read *Sea of Cortez*, I realized that sometimes Steinbeck went back to writing fiction.

En route we ran into a little dugout canoe full of Indians. I guess they were Seri Indians. We had heard about them and they were supposed to be cannibals. We asked them where they were going and they said, "La Paz." We asked them, "You want a tow to town?" They said, "Yeah, okay." They were dressed in normal clothes and didn't look that different, or even like cannibals. One of them wanted to sell us some gold nuggets.

There was an old lady in the boat and she kept her shawl over her mouth. So we didn't know if she was afraid of malaria or what. Every time we came across some people Steinbeck would ask, "Is there any malaria here?" They would always answer, "No, the next town, the next town." We didn't have any malaria shots or medicine with us. Luckily, no one became sick during our trip except "Doc" who got terribly seasick on the return trip. Of course I'm not counting a lot of hangovers.

The Indians were trying to sell us pearls in a little box, but we didn't care for them. The oysters had a disease eight or so years before that and had just petered out. The oyster shells were thick with disease. In that area at the time there were lots of myths about boys finding pearls of great value and throwing them back into the sea. Maybe that's where Steinbeck got his idea for *The Pearl*. He never talked about it, though, on the trip.

Anyhow we gave the Indians back their pearls, but the two men did come on board. We gave them some apples and oranges and some glasses of wine. So we towed them for awhile, but we were stopping at Espiritu Sancto Island and they were heading for La Paz, so we set them adrift and they went away.

None of the strangers we invited on board ever made us feel afraid. We always felt safe on board and maybe that's because our boat had been blessed. In September every year at the Feast of Santa Rosalia all the boats would be decorated with flowers and flags for the blessing. One year we decorated The Eneas, my father's boat, with thousands of begonias against a background of wild fern because I knew a flower shop owner who donated them to us. Some of the other boats had religious statues and flags of all kinds. The parade of boats which lasted about an hour was a beautiful sight.

We would move the boat alongside the wharf and the local bishop would bless every boat. Then we would parade through Alvarado Street to the Customhouse Plaza en route to the church. The men would carry the patron saint of Sicily. There would be a few floats and the Queen and her escorts. Men and women dressed in costumes and carried flags. We would sing the Star Spangled Banner and have a few minutes of prayer. There was food galore—squid, pizza, Italian sausage, cannellonis, spaghetti and different kinds of pastries. Everybody would dance until dark before going back to the boats. Those were the good ol' days!

"Tiny" and I had never seen manta rays before. We had two or three Mexican harpoons with us and "Tiny" was determined to spear one of the giant rays. They were huge—about twenty-five or thirty feet across. They were just too big, and they kept breaking our lines. We just couldn't hold onto 'em. Steinbeck would ask "Tiny", "What's so important about harpooning a manta ray?" Well, we just wanted to get one and take a picture of it to prove we could do it, but they were too strong for us.

After we anchored in the bay we could see schools of fish swiming around. Although it was dark, they were phosphorescent and showed up like there was light in the water. We had a small lampara net on the skiff so we circled the fish with the net and pulled both ends tight to catch them. Each time we could see the fish in the circle but every time we pulled it in there were no fish.

Captain Berry yelled at us, "What kind of fish did you get?" We yelled back that we had "made skunk" which, in fisherman's language means that we didn't catch anything. Then he kidded back to us, "Do you need a fish captain?"

That made us mad so we tried putting in the net three more times. We had no luck even though we could see the fish on the outside of the net. It finally dawned on us that the fish must be real small and were slipping through the mesh. By this time "Tex" and Captain Berry were razzing us that we were "bum fishermen."

That made "Tiny" and me even madder so we turned on all the deck lights to attract the fish to the boat. Then we pulled out a dip net with a smaller mesh. Within minutes we had the net full of fish-little sardines, anchovies, and mackerel. They averaged about one and a half inches long. That satisfied us that we were good fishermen after all because it wasn't our fault that the fish had been so small that they slipped through our net.

I put on a big frying pan with some olive oil on the stove. We sprinkled salt and pepper on them and they were delicious. It was just like eating peanuts. We poured ourselves a couple of glasses of wine and we gorged ourselves. Then we settled into one of our nightly bull sessions. The beaches were beautiful on Espiritu Sancto Island. We must have found at least fifty different kinds of specimens. We caught a yellow fin tuna and Steinbeck raved about the way I cooked it—with a tomato sauce of onions and spices. At night a Mexican guy came by and wanted to sell us a big sea bass. So we had plenty of good, fresh fish.

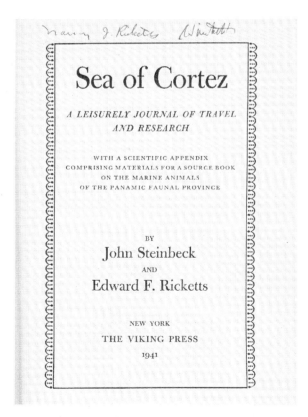

Autographed title page to Steinbeck's book. Courtesy Steinbeck Archives, Salinas Public Library, Salinas CA.>

At night the wind came down so we moved from Espiritu Sancto on to the mainland, which was about a mile away. From there we were going to La Paz. "Tiny" and I had the watch from 3 a.m. to 6 a.m. and that's when we ran into trouble with the mirage. Because of it we couldn't estimate how far away the land was so that threw our timing off, too.

We could see a light on the left side of the island and we figured it could be a lighthouse or a tuna boat drifting with the mast light on. That island looked like it was just an hour away. "Tiny" said, "Jesus! Something must be wrong. We're supposed to be there by 7:30 A.M. and it's only 3:30. What do you think? I'd better call Captain Berry."

Captain Berry said, "Either you guys are off course or you've discovered a new island." We had some coffee with him and he asked us, "You're sure you have the right course?" "Yeah", we answered. "We may be a degree off, but that's all. "So, You're all right", he says and goes back to sleep.

John Steinbeck (left) Captain Tony Berry right.
Photo Sparky Enea

So all night it was travel, travel, travel. By God, we got there at just about 7:30 or 8:00 in the morning even though it had looked only an hour away. We thought something was wrong, but it was only a mirage. The same thing happened to me when I was overseas in North Africa during the war. Something looked just a few miles away and it was hours away. Mirages are tricky things. Sometimes you visualize islands or buildings or it may even look like a town in the distance. So, in spite of what Steinbeck said in the book, "Tiny" and I were never really off course.

While we were in Espiritu Sancto Island, we saw a beautiful black yacht go by. It had an awning over the deck and the ladies and gentlemen on it were dressed in white clothes. We saw it again when we got to Guaymas.

I wish to Christ "Tiny" was still alive. He could tell you more stories than I can about what he was involved in. You know, he was only an inch taller than me, but he had wavy hair and there was something about him that women loved. He'd have about four or five girls at one time. I'd be nice to 'em, dance with 'em, but they would never have anything to do with me when he was around.

Tiny's love affairs with women were legendary among his friends. I remember that he went around with at least three girls from Flora's at different times. Even at his funeral, his friends laughed about all his romantic adventures. We started to remember them and then we would tell the old stories again and start to laugh. It was the only funeral that I've ever been to that was like that.

The main thing we remembered was that the great thing about "Tiny" was that he never felt guilty about anything. He was about ready to prove that again once we hit La Paz!

LA PAZ

This was it—La Paz—the part we all had been waiting for! "Tiny" and I were shaving, bathing, and putting on clean clothes while the port pilot came out to steer the Western Flyer down the channel to Prieta Point. We put on white shirts and levis. Steinbeck made a few mistakes when he wrote about La Paz in *The Sea of Cortez*. First of all, he says we went to church on Good Friday and I double-checked with Captain Berry and it was Easter Sunday, two days later.

Then he says that "Tex" went into town with me and Tiny. "Now, that's wrong." "Tiny" and I had plans to head for the whorehouses. "Tex" was engaged and wasn't interested in our plans. Like I say, "Tiny" and I were single and we were ready to find a girl.

We were never ashamed of what we did in different ports. When Steinbeck would question us we would tell him, "We are only human and we are doing what we have to do. After all we are single and in the prime of life." Every time we said it, Steinbeck would roar with laughter.

Carol came out on deck all dressed up in a skirt, sweater, and yellow shoes. We stepped onto the boat where the immigration officials were checking our passports and Carol came on, too. She asked us when we got off in the boat, "Well, where are you guys going?" We said, "Oh, we're going here and there." "Well, can I come with you?" She asked. "Forget about it," we said. So she went one way and we went another. In fact, the whole crew went off in different directions.

"Tiny" and I went into a few whorehouses, but they kept telling us, "No way. It's Good Friday. The girls won't work between 12:00 and 3:00 P.M." That's how I remembered for sure that we landed in La Paz on Good Friday.

So "Tiny" and I kept walking around. There were a couple of old buildings there made out of adobe and we heard voices. We looked in and there were two couples and mattresses. The dirt floor was real hard, like cement and there were real clean mattresses there with white sheets and pillows. We peeked in and said, "Como estas, hombre. Hey, what's cookin'?" That's how we found out it was two girls and their pimps. We asked if we could take on the girls, but they said, "No, not until 3:00."

So we said, "Can we get a drink, then?" One guy says, "Well, if you give me some money I'll buy a bottle of tequilla." When he came back, we found out it was cheap, just thirty or forty cents a bottle, so the six of us started drinking it. Then we bought another one and we were all feeling pretty good in that heat. "Tiny" says, "Jeez, at least after two bottles we should get something out of these girls."

We knew a little Spanish so we approached the girls ourselves. They whispered among themselves and decided to break the Good Friday rules. We mentioned two pesos which was about eighteen cents but they asked for three pesos which we agreed to.

The heat was about ninety degrees or more and after two bottles of tequilla, "Tiny" and I were feeling pretty high. The abandoned house had two rooms so we put one mattress in the other room. After we'd had our fun, the pimps asked us to buy another bottle of tequilla but we told them we had to meet some people soon. We told the girls we'd see them later on and left.

Well, we finally got out of there and headed back to the boat. Just as were heading back to the boat here comes Carol, loaded. We were all gassed up and hot, so we went into the boat to get our swimming trunks. We had hired an old Mexican guy to guard the boat and keep the kids away. We dove into the water to cool off a little and Carol asked us, "How's the water?" "Jesus, it's beautiful, nice and warm," I said.

Tiny, living it up in La Paz!
Courtesy, Sparky Enea

But we never expected her to throw herself into the water, clothes and all. Now you can imagine the three of us all gassed up trying to swim. Thank God we had an old tire on the boat. We threw it to her, but we had a helluva time pulling her back on the boat all soaking wet.

When she gets back on board, she's just got a sweater on, no brassiere. She took her sweater off and when the old Mexican saw her nude to the waist he went to the bow of the boat.

I said to her, because we didn't know each other too good at the time, "Carol, don't ever do that again. Now get in there and change your clothes."

"To "Tiny" I said, "Tiny", I don't like this. Let's change our clothes and go meet the rest of the crew." If I hadn't spoken up, I think something would have happened between Carol and "Tiny" right then and there.

Carol was a nice looking girl at this time. She was about five foot seven and well built. Her hair was long and brown and mostly she wore shorts on board ship. "Tiny" was interested in getting into her.

So "Tiny" and I changed into our clothes again and headed for shore. We met the rest of the crew in town and we ate tuna tacos and drank Carta Blanca beer. Carol had embarrassed me. It seemed to me that she was just interested in getting laid. After that we tried to stay away from her. When Carol dove overboard she was wearing an expensive watch that Steinbeck had given her—maybe worth three or four hundred dollars. The next day after breakfast she pretended to slip over the guard rail and fall into the water. Then she told Steinbeck, "Now my watch isn't working. "That's how she could explain her ruined watch. Steinbeck took her into town to a jewelry store to get her watch fixed.

The rate of exchange for the peso was so good that we bought lots of souvenirs: shawls, carved cow horns and colored handkerchiefs. We loved buying the big turtle shells. Later on I gave mine to the Garcia family who opened a Mexican restaurant in Monterey. "Tiny" traded his for a carton of cigarettes but Captain Tony Berry still has his. Of everything I guess the stuffed turtle shells turned out to be our favorite souvenirs.

On Easter Sunday we went to Mass in a beautiful church in La Paz. We stayed for the whole service. I had been brought up a Catholic, but I had never seen a Mass like this in a foreign country. The whole crew enjoyed the ceremony and the singing and we stayed until the end of it. There was a lot of singing and the choir marched down the aisles and around the altar. It lasted over an hour and even Steinbeck was impressed. It was beautiful!

Afterwards we went out for a few drinks and Carol decided we should buy some fresh meat. She wanted to buy some flank steaks that were under some wire and covered with flies. Carol was ready to buy them until Captain Berry said, "Carol, I wouldn't serve those to my dog."

Then we passed an old house that had some chickens and roosters in the front yard. Carol says, "I wonder if they'd sell us some?" We knocked on the door and an old Mexican lady says, "Well, if you can catch one, we'll sell it to you. Okay?" Just visualize two drunk guys, in about ninety degree weather, trying to catch this rooster. The yard was small and enclosed. The rooster kept cackling all the time and the chickens were screaming. I don't remember how many times we fell down but Carol kept egging us on. "Tiny" and I were laughing the whole time and the whole family came out to watch us. Carol paid a dollar for it and we took it back to the boat. I killed it, feathered it and cleaned it. Then I made chicken and dumplings for us for supper. It was too much for one meal so I put the rest of it on ice.

While in La Paz we had collected on El Mogote, a sandy peninsula. There we ran into a poisonous little fish called the botete. We had never seen anything like it. The liver of this fish is used to kill flies. You take the liver out and it attracts flies like fly paper. When they eat it, they die.

As we left La Paz, the day after Easter, we wondered what other surprises lay ahead of us—animal and human—on the rest of our islands. The next big stop would be Guaymas, but in between we planned to do some collecting on several other islands like Cayo and San Jose and the Marcial Reef. Each proved fascinating in their own way.

SMALL STOPS; SAN JOSE, ESCONDIDO, LORETO, CONCEPCION BAY, ANGEL DE LA GUARDIA

The next morning we sailed early towards San Jose Island, our next collecting station, but mid-afternoon we stopped at a small islet called Cayo on the southwest tip.

San Jose Island was spooky. We didn't hear anything on it—no birds or nothing. We all said, "There's something wrong here some place. It's too quiet."

I did find one beautiful thing there, though. On these small islands the beaches are full of shells. My God, there must have been about fifty or sixty varieties. So I started to pick up the seashells and put them into the flour sacks that we had on the boat.

Everyone thought I was nuts. Steinbeck asked me, "What are you goin' to do with them?" I said, "Well, Jeez, they look pretty." So all during the trip after that, every island or beach we went to I collected seashells. By the end of the trip I had collected about twelve sacks.

But we were right in feeling uneasy about that island. All of a sudden we were attacked by hordes of small, black flies. I guess they were gnats. Even when we dressed, the little bugs would get down our clothes. There was no way to fight them except to get the hell out of there as fast as we could. Captain Berry got the boat out of there quickly and we were free of that plague about five miles later. It had been an awful fright!

Since it was necessary to flee the scene to escape the flies, we headed up the coast toward Marcial Reef. We didn't get good tides there, so when that happened we did some of our collecting after dark. We used big seven-cell battery flashlights so that we could see what we were collecting. On Marcial Reef we found one huge lobster. It was the only one we saw during the entire trip.

While we were collecting there, "Tiny" was rowing in the little skiff. We heard him shout and then we saw a giant manta ray heading towards him. "Harpoon him", I shouted but he was too frozen with fear. It could have flicked "Tiny" and the boat with one flap of its giant wing. There was real danger for a moment! He started swearing and then just sat quietly in the boat. He made up his mind once again to catch and kill one of the giant manta rays.

From there we sailed on to Puerto Escondido, which is a gorgeous place with two harbors and mountains on both sides. One of the harbors is so narrow that it could only contain one rowboat. That's why it got the name of "hidden harbor."

When we got there, these two Mexican officials came over on two black horses. They waved to us so we went to shore to pick them up. They were from Loreto and they loved to hunt the big, wild sheep up in the hills. We brought them on the boat and we gave them cigarettes and a little canned fruit.

They told us they were going hunting overnight and they asked us, "Would anybody like to go?" "Doc" Ricketts said, "Yeah, we'd like to go." So I packed them a lunch and they went off overnight.

Then about 5:30 in the morning, I looked over and "Tiny" was just getting into his bunk. I woke up and said, "What's the matter?" "Jeez", he answered. "They almost caught me in the act." Then I looked out the porthole and saw these two Mexican guys. I had asked them to bring fresh tomatoes and cabbage to us.

Tony woke up at that time because he heard us talking. Just then I heard Carol's door close, and I guess he heard it, too. I didn't ask any questions.

The next day "Doc" and Steinbeck returned with two packhorses. None of them had killed any bighorn sheep. They were tired and a little disappointed but they told us that they had seen some really beautiful country. They brought back about five or six cases of beer with them.

Tiny in the bow of the Western Flyer. He hunted the manta rays
with relentless passion. Doc and Steinbeck were on the
Japanese shrimp boats.
Courtesy, Sparky Enea

I made a big plate of spaghetti for all of them to eat. The whole crew was excited about going back to Puerto Escondido because, not only was it beautiful, but it was also one of the places where we found the most specimens. In only nine days of collecting, we had almost a boat full of specimens. We had plenty of formaldehyde with us and never ran out for the entire trip. John, Carol and "Doc" would drop the fish into little vials, look them up in their books, and mark them right away. And we didn't kill ourselves with work. In between collecting we laughed, played, told stories, ate big meals and drank lots of beer.

Next we sailed for Loreto and we could see through our glasses that it was a stretch of sandy beach about three or four miles long. There weren't any coves so we just dropped anchor about five hundred yards off the beach. Loreto is not a place that is visited very often by foreigners, so their officials got all dressed up to come out to meet us when we dropped anchor. Everyone put on clean shirts and I sprinkled the crew with shaving lotion.

When we dropped anchor and went on land, all the people stared at us. As we passed by we could hear them giggle behind our backs. Most of all we wanted to see the mission as it is supposed to be the oldest mission in the western hemisphere. On the ground in front of the mission were these wonderful heavy old mission bells. The mission was really rundown. Everything was overgrown and needed paint and repair work. I talked to some people, though, who went there recently and they told me that the bells are back up and the mission is now completely restored. "Tiny" decided that he wanted to steal a few of the bells. He had a plan for getting some ropes to tow them out to the boat. I refused to go along with him. I said, "Tiny", are you crazy? If the Mexicans catch us, they'll put us in jail and throw away the key." So "Tiny" gave up the idea.

This place was so remote that we couldn't talk to any of our fishermen friends back in Monterey on the boat radio. Nobody on board was even interested in playing cards. We just liked to drink and go back to our bull sessions. In addition to our talk about Flora's girls, we also knew a lot of the guys, for instance, who had sold cats to "Doc" for twenty-five cents apiece. The kids sold them to him and he would sell them to college and biological labs. Twenty-five cents in 1928 or 1929 was big money in those days. That was more money than their parents earned in an hour at the cannery. Some of those guys are dead now but sometimes I run into those old men in some of the Monterey bars.

Then sometimes we'd talk about the cannery workers on the Row. Some of the husbands and wives worked different shifts. Other women were married to fishermen and they wouldn't see their husbands for a few days at a time. So there was a lot of lovemaking in cars and sometimes in a big old boiler that was in the lot next to Wing Chong's and across from Doc's lab. Some cannery workers went inside for a little love affair or maybe a drink. It was about thirty feet long. Maybe even some cannery workers slept there when they were down and out and first came to work in the canneries. They would make love in the boiler when they had a few hours off, but nobody ever lived there as far as I know like Steinbeck wrote in *Sweet Thursday*.

After collecting on Coronado we started the engines up again and moved toward Concepcion Bay. Everything was lovely, the beaches, the pelicans and especially the shells. I collected some more shells here and yet, when I got back home, I gave them all away to all my friends except one sack. On the way back when we got to customs, they asked, "What are they worth?" "Hell, they're souvenirs," I argued. So they only charged me about five dollars.

When I got married, I left that bag of shells in my father's cellar. One day a vendor came along and he sold the bag for twenty dollars. He didn't know. He thought it was a good deal, but now I don't have a single shell left. After the trip my brother, who worked at the Monterey Bank, set up a little exhibit that said, SHELLS FROM THE STEINBECK/RICKETTS EXPEDITION TO THE SEA OF CORTEZ.

In Concepcion Bay we also found some unusual sponges, maroon in color, about as big as a doughnut with a hole in the middle. We also caught a small octopus there. A Mexican guy, who worked for a British gold mine asked us if we wanted to buy gold nuggets. Then he said, "What are you guys doing here?" "We're collecting specimens," we answered.

He looked as if suddenly we might be of use to him. There was a presidential election down there at the time and he was expecting trouble. So he asked us if we had any bullets. Then Steinbeck asked him how the election was coming out. John whispered to us, "If these guys ask for bullets, tell them you don't even have a gun."

Angel de la Guardia was the last island we went to. I harpooned a red snapper there. There's no real red snapper in California. We use the wrong name. It's really a type of rock cod. Red snappers are found only in Mexico or on the East Coast. This one was about three and a half feet, orange in color and I scaled it and filleted it. It was pure white meat and I baked it with garlic, parsley, onion, potato and tomato sauce. It was out of this world!

The next stop was Tiburon Island. That's where I harpooned the bat. Steinbeck couldn't stop laughing over this incident and made a big story out of it for everyone. Next we stopped at San Francisco Island which had a nice cove where we could anchor for the night before going on

This was the first island where "Tiny" felt a little sick. It turned out to be only a little gas. But we were both getting restless to get to a big port again. The next was Guaymas and we could hardly wait!

GUAYMAS

When we got to Guaymas, we felt like we had gotten back to civilization. There were businesses there and communications like newspapers and telegrams. It was like being "in touch" again. We saw the black yacht for the second time and lots of other grand boats for the sports fishermen. Best of all we knew that the whorehouses there were a dime a dozen. Some of the best adventures from our trip happened here.

One of the first people we met in Guaymas was Captain Corona. I remembered hearing that name from my father. So I said to him, "You know, in 1921 my father, brother, and cousin came down here to fish for shrimp." Captain Corona answered, "Oh, yeah. I remember, they had a little boat, but they didn't catch much shrimp because they had the wrong kind of net." Dried shrimp were getting a big price at that time. They had a small boat, but the Mexicans told them where the shrimp were and they fished near a river town called Tapolobanho. My dad sent home about one hundred pounds—nice big prawns big, solid and dried. We just wolfed them down!

Then Captain Corona said, "Hey, we're having boxing matches tonight. Do you want to come?" Then Steinbeck replied, "Well, we've got a Navy boxing champion on board our ship." So Captain Corona said, "Well, let's fix up a fight," and they did.

Now "Tiny" was about my size, maybe an inch taller. In 1933 while he was in the Navy he won the bantamweight boxing championship during the Long Beach earthquake. He was 118 pounds. He had fought for about four years, but he had never won the championship before because he couldn't stay in condition. There was a prize fighter by the name of Johnny Buff. He told "Tiny", "If you want to win the title, you've got to train and lay off the booze and women." "Tiny" listened to him for awhile and finally he won the All-Navy Championship.

"Tiny" and I had been boxing partners since we were about twelve or thirteen years old. His backyard and my backyard met, so we had been neighbors since we were kids. We used to fight exhibition fights at the Elks Lodge, the Hotel Del Monte on the polo fields. The members used to throw change at us—nickels, dimes and quarters. Once we collected $26 and thought we were rich even though we always gave the money to our folks.

"Tiny" agreed to an exhibition fight that night, but then we had a rough afternoon. There was a yacht called the Florinda in the harbor and "Tex", our engineer, knew their engineer. He came over with a gallon of Bacardi rum and I started frying up some shrimps. The heat was about one hundred degrees. "Tiny" started drinking and I said, "Tiny", you're supposed to fight an exhibition tonight." "Don't worry about it," he answered. He just ignored me and kept drinking all afternoon.

When we got to the arena we found out that the guy "Tiny" is supposed to fight was about 5'7" and called "Kid Senorita." The posters were saying that "Kid Senorita" had knocked out this guy and that guy.

Now this was supposed to be a three-round exhibition. I was Tiny's second, so when we got into the ring, I said, "Three rounds." They said, "No, no", because they wanted four. Finally I agreed, but "Tiny" didn't know it. "Tiny" looked good in the first round. He's strong and clever. "Kid Senorita" was 5'5" and "Tiny" was 5'2". "Tiny" weighed about 125 lbs and the "Kid" weighed about 135 lbs. He danced around the "Kid" and got in some quick jabs to the face and chest. There were a lot of Americans in the audience and they applauded. Steinbeck started betting money on him. The second worked out, too. He looked really good.

Then in the third round "Tiny" tells me, "Well, I think I'll try to knock this guy out." "No", I told him. "Don't try to knock him out. Just box with him."

"Tiny" figured the third round was his last round, so he got a little cute and fancy. "Tiny" was half-bombed and he tried to rush the "Kid" and knock him against the ropes. I kept hollering at "Tiny" to stay away from him and just box. He charged him and hit him. The second time the "Kid" sidestepped and "Tiny" hit the ropes. When he hit the ropes, "Kid Senorita" clobbered him. So the round ended and "Tiny" figured it was over. "No, you gotta go one more round." I said to him,

Well, "Tiny" tried to get clever again and this Mexican guy really hit him. He fell and hit his head on the floor and there was no matting. The Mexican crowd went crazy. I tell you, I thought he had killed "Tiny." So I took the towel to him and said, "Tiny", how are you?" He opened one eye and said, "You son of a bitch. You double-crossed me." Then I knew he was okay.

When he went to take a shower, the "Kid" said to me, "Boy, your friend smells of booze. "I said, "Yes, he was a little drunk." If he was sober, I think "Tiny" could have knocked the "Kid" out. He only hit "Tiny" with one punch but it was a good one. Later we went to the whorehouses so I knew there was nothing wrong with my friend.

The next morning "Tiny" and I went to town to buy some souvenirs. Guaymas was really loaded with all sorts of souvenir shops. We came to a clothing store whose owner was Yugoslavian and Captain Tony Berry is a Yugoslavian, so they became friends. He said, "We're going to have a big turtle dinner with some big shots from the Japanese shrimp fleet. Would you guys like to come?"

We said, "Yeah" and around one o'clock we went to one of those bars with the long verandahs. That's the place where we watched them kill and prepare the turtle meat. Now we knew what we had done wrong!

The beer and whiskey were flowing and, through interpreters, the Japanese were asking, "What are you guys down here for?" I could speak a little Spanish, so I explained to them "scientific expedition." Captain Berry noticed the Japanese pouring whiskey into my glass when I wasn't looking. So he said to me, "Sparky, do you speak pig Latin?" When I said, "Yes", he told me, "This guy is trying to get you drunk." So I stopped drinking.

I guess they thought we were spies. You see, it was 1940. Besides fishing for shrimp, they were down there getting the lay of the land for war. They knew it was going to happen, but we didn't. You've got to put two and two together.

After that "Tiny" and I made the rounds of the whorehouses. We really loved Guaymas and were talking about living there. Tony and "Tex" were really homesick by now and the rest of the crew also seemed anxious to get home. Later many of our friends asked about the girls. We said it was better in La Paz and Guaymas than in Monterey and the red light district was mostly out of town—all night clubs, just like Alvarado. At one time Alvarado Street had twenty-two bars. In La Paz and Guaymas they had bars and girls for sale. They had juke box music at night, live music—all young girls. Oldest might be twenty-two years old.

The exchange at that time was twelve pesos for an American dollar. The price of taking a girl in her room was about eighteen cents. After taking one of the girls, we drank and danced. After about an hour we decided to take on different girls, so we danced and talked to the other girls. They have rules where and when you have an affair. You must stay with one girl during the time you are in the bar so we decided to go onto another club, and so on. After three different places we decided to go and have something to eat. We didn't want to take the chance of eating Mexican food at that time. In each town you go they have at least ten or fifteen whorehouses or night clubs, whichever you want to call them.

By eight o'clock we'd had our belly full and so we decided to go back to the boat. We were surprised to hear music and saw that there were two guitar players on board. Everyone asked us, "Where have you been?" and we said, "Here and there."

As we found out, the rest of them had eaten in a Mexican restaurant and brought two waitresses and the guitar players back with them. Everyone was singing and I sat alongside one of the Mexican girls at a galley table that was alongside one of the galley walls. Carol was in the middle and a Mexican official was on the other side. Everyone was there and they said, "See what you missed. Two beautiful Mexican girls!"

Well I can speak a little Spanish and we were all feeling good, so I put my hand on the girl's thigh. I was feeling her up and she wasn't saying nothing. Carol was sitting on the other side of the girl. I felt a hand grab mine and I thought it was the Mexican girl. Then I noticed that the girl's hand was on the table.

Captain Berry noticed the whole situation and said, "Carol, for Crissake, give "Sparky" a break. Your kind are a dime a dozen."

Steinbeck had seen the whole thing, too and he jumped up and said, "You can't say that against my wife." Tony took a swing at John. We all got up. "Tex" grabbed John and I grabbed Tony. A few more words were said and then it was all over. No blows were struck.

No one mentioned the incident again but the strain between Steinbeck and Captain Berry lasted until we left San Diego and were en route home.

SAN DIEGO AGAIN!

On Monday morning we sailed out of Guaymas again with Captain Corona as our guide. In less than an hour we came across the Japanese fishing fleet. We saw a terrific catch on board their ship that we, as fellow fishermen, really envied. The Japanese fishermen were only interested in their shrimp haul. When John and "Doc" saw all those fish, they took the skiff over to one of the dredge boats and asked permission to board. The Captain was most polite and showed them the catch of the day. While the crew stood by and watched, John and "Doc" started to scoop up various fish for their collection.

Since the Japanese were only interested in the shrimp, they threw overboard all the rest of the fish. I watched in horror as we saw tons of good fish being thrown overboard—sandabs, sole, anchovies, sardines, mackerel—you name it. When John and "Doc" came back, they were happy about showing us all their new specimens. I was glad for them but I was disgusted that they hadn't brought back any fresh fish for me to cook. What a waste!

Then we saw a bunch of manta rays again. "Tiny" grabbed the harpoon. A manta ray is a very frightening adversary. It has a wing span of between twenty and thirty feet. After you harpoon one, you need to attach it to a buoy so it can thrash around for awhile. The point is to tire the manta ray out before you can bring it in. They kept looming over Tiny's head but he didn't have any buoys to work them with. What a struggle! He speared a couple of them, but the lines always broke under the weight of the big fish. So "Tiny" was heartbroken again over not getting his manta ray. He was afraid that none of our friends in Monterey would ever believe that he had actually speared one without a picture.

On the way home we stopped at Agiabampo. "Tiny" and I rowed "Doc", Carol and John into the lagoon. This would be one of our last collecting spots before we left the Gulf and headed home.

It was then that we ran into the last and only storm on our trip. When the storm came up, we were hugging the coastline pretty tightly. There shouldn't have been a problem but we were lighter than usual in fuel and water. Around Port Eugene, about ten hours above Cape San Lucas, we hit the open sea. Big waves rocked us and we started bouncing around like a cork in a bottle. We rode it out. It lasted for three days and I didn't have a chance to cook for those three days. I just made sandwiches and coffee for everybody.

None of us got sick except "Doc." He got terribly seasick and never left his bunk. We took his wheel watches for him. He took all kinds of pills but nothing seemed to help. He just lay in his bunk.

Once when it was time for his wheel watch "Tiny" went in to try and wake him up. "Tiny" said to me, "He looks like he's dead. With that beard he looks like Jesus Christ!" So he opened one eye and said, "No, I'm not Jesus Christ. I'm only half dead."

We also felt better because now we could start using the telephone on the boat. Our fishermen friends started calling us up to see if any tuna were jumping. Steinbeck called his friend, Spencer Tracy, to see if he could meet us in San Diego. "Tiny" called up Dawn, one of Flora's girls, that he was going around with at this time and told her to meet him in San Diego with his car.

For the first time we turned on the radio to listen to the news. We were all surprised to hear about the invasion of Norway. Steinbeck kept the news station on and kept taking notes like mad. When we got to San Diego he bought every paper he could to read about it. About a month after we got back he had already finished writing *The Moon Is Down.*

Edward "Doc" Ricketts in his lab. (1937) Brian Fitch, Courtesy of the Steinbeck Archives, Salinas Public Library, Salinas CA.

When we got to Immigration in San Diego we had another disappointment. John got real friendly with the immigration official when he heard that he had gone to Stanford, too. He asked John to autograph a copy of Grapes and he did. Then the guy pointed to the bottle of Damiana and asked, "What's that?" Then he told us we couldn't take it in. Steinbeck asked, "Well, can we drink it here?" "Too late", was the answer. John stormed off the boat saying, "You're no Stanford graduate." "Tex", after he heard that news, went below deck and drank some of his gallon of Bacardi rum and broke the rest of it before it could be confiscated.

In San Diego, Steinbeck invited me and "Tiny" to a steak dinner at the San Diego Hotel. Then he told us, "And I'm not going to invite Tony or "Tex." We thought it was real cheap of him not to invite them. I guess he was still mad about the fight.

Steinbeck still didn't want to pay "Tiny" any money until Captain Tony Berry reminded him how hard "Tiny" had worked, even taking wheel shifts. The value of the specimens we had collected made us feel he should have given us a bonus. Spencer Tracy didn't show up. He called from San Luis Obispo to say that he was tied up on a picture.

Max Wagner came down to meet us instead. He was a Hollywood character actor and an old neighbor of John's from Salinas. He was a character in real life, too. For example, if we went into a bar, Max would always sit on the floor rather than on a stool or table. That's how he liked to drink and talk. He always told a lot of jokes, too.

After dinner we went into a back room. Two women were sitting at the bar and they could hear us laughing and talking in there. "Tiny" talked to them and told them, "That's John Steinbeck in there. He wrote *The Grapes of Wrath* and he's just getting back from Mexico."

John told "Tiny", "Ask the girls if they want to come in and have a drink." We had three or four drinks and one of the girls whispered to me, "I'm gonna ask him for an autograph." I told her, "Hell, no, he doesn't like that." But she went ahead and asked him anyway.

So John said, "Well, aren't you girls having a good time? Why do you want an autograph?" They kept asking him until he finally said, "Okay, I'll give you an autograph, but then get the hell out of here." Then he called a cab and we went to some other place. He hated any kind of publicity.

"Tiny" and his girl, Dawn, stayed overnight at a nearby hotel. Carol and John stayed there, too. "Doc" and I headed back to the boat. The next day "Doc" went up to "Tiny" and asked him if he'd mind if he rode home with Dawn in the car. I guess he was tired of being seasick and didn't want to stay on the boat any longer. "It's okay with me", "Tiny" told him. You should have seen the smile on Doc's face. He was thrilled to get off the boat, get in that shiny roadster and drive off with a pretty girl.

When Carol heard that she got really mad. She went into her stateroom and slammed the door. To this day I never figured out why she was mad. Was she mad at "Tiny" because he invited his girlfriend down there? Or was she mad at "Doc" because he went home with Tiny's girl?

We didn't see much of Carol after San Diego on the trip back to Monterey. I was still doing the cooking and the weather was still rough. Even though we didn't see her much, we knew that when two of us were on wheel watch and three were sleeping, she would sneak into the galley and get something to eat. We finally dropped anchor at San Simeon at two thirty in the morning.

By five the wind had settled down a bit so we could continue on our way. On the deck we kept a big barrel of fresh fish near the stern. We had bonito and striped tuna for our friends. We were keeping it salted, but everybody started putting salt into it. By the time we got to Monterey it was so goddammed salty we had to throw the whole thing overboard.

When we docked in Monterey in the morning it seemed as if everyone was there to meet us. The dock was full of people. I started giving my shells to friends and pretty soon I only had one bag left for myself. All our friends started asking us questions about the Mexican whorehouses. Pretty soon it started to feel like one big party.

Everyone was sorry to see the trip end. We all felt that the six weeks had gone too quickly. Finally we accepted it because as "Tiny" said, "Nothing lasts. Everything has to end." But we didn't need another party. We were just getting back from a six-week party in the Sea of Cortez!

A POSTSCRIPT FOR THE TRIP

The day in April that marked the end of our famous trip to the Sea of Cortez did not mean the end of our friendship with all the people on it. We discussed the possibility of a future trip to the Aleutians. If "Doc" and Steinbeck had gone, it's a sure bet that "Tiny" and I would have gone along, too. But World War II came along and John became more famous and moved to New York. Then "Doc" got killed when the Del Monte Express hit his car, so that ended that.

A couple of weeks after we got back from the trip my sister said, "Why don't you invite all the crew over for a spaghetti dinner?" So everyone came over to the house and my dad says, "Hi, Doctor?" Ricketts answered, "Oh, Mr. Enea. I didn't connect you and "Sparky." My dad had been Secretary/Treasurer for the boat owners' union, so when "Doc" came to town he had asked my dad if the fishermen caught any rare fish to call him up. The funny thing is that they had known each other for years.

Another time we ran into "Doc" and John when Carol was out of town. "Tiny" and I had been going to a nightclub called the Colony Club. Drinks were only twenty-five cents so you could get drunk on a couple of bucks. There was dancing and entertainment. There was a big blonde girl there—sort of an Amazon—who did an act with a big, black snake.

Doc Ricketts in his lab showing a snake to a young visitor. The lab
was the setting for Steinbeck's story "The Snake."

59

John had been out of town and he asked us, "What's new?" "Tiny" told him that "There's a big, beautiful blonde Amazon down at the Colony Club." We used to talk to her and dance with her. So John and "Doc" came down to the Club and we introduced them to her. John got acquainted with her and told her that I had cooked spaghetti on the boat. I had cooked spaghetti that afternoon, so John said, "Let's all go down to the lab and have some."

*800 Cannery Row in Monterrey where Doc Ricketts
lived and worked.*

So all five of us went down to the lab. We ate the spaghetti, had a few drinks, and started throwing the bull. I could see that John and "Doc" had big eyes for her. Finally I whispered to "Tiny", "There are four men and one girl. That's too many. We better go."

They said, "Where are you guys going?" "Someplace." So we left and what happened after that I never did ask. I never did ask too many questions, but I know John and "Doc" were definitely a couple of "studs."

When John moved up to his house in the Santa Cruz mountains in Los Gatos, he invited all of us to a party. It was an old country house, but it had a guest house and a swimming pool. The furniture was old and the decor was nothing special. But the view was magnificent because we could see the whole Santa Clara Valley from there.

Charlie Chaplin was coming up from Hollywood and John had been bragging about my spaghetti. He asked me if I would cook up some spaghetti for Spencer Tracy and I said, "Yes."

John told us it would be a big barbecue maybe fifty or seventy-five people. That weekend we were visiting some relatives in Pittsburg, California, so we decided to go over on Saturday night.

We were all dancing and John kept going by and asking me if I knew where Carol was. He said, "It's a full moon and that's when she starts thinking about the birds and the bees."

I was dancing with a girl who looked like she was dressed in blue pajamas. "John," I answered, "It's gettin' late. I'll take this girl down to show her the pool. Maybe Carol is down there." So I put my arm around this girl and walked towards the pool.It was about twenty yards. All the time I'm kissing her and feeling her up. Then I heard voices down at the end of the pool where it's dark. All at once I heard footsteps and I called out, "Tiny, Tiny." In a split second there's a light on and there was "Tiny" sitting in a wicker chair. Carol is sitting on his lap with her blouse undone. John says, "This nonsense has gone far enough." "Tiny" answered, "Yeah, John, we're getting ready to leave."

We were sleeping in the guest house and when "Tiny" got back to it, I said, "Tiny", what the hell are you doin'?" "Aw, don't worry about it", "Tiny" answered. "I'm going to kill that bastard." He didn't say anything more and we just went to bed.

The next morning around seven, Steinbeck came to the guest house to wake us up. He told us that Spencer Tracy and his agent were down at the house and wanted to meet us. I put on trunks and went down to be introduced. Spencer Tracy said to me, "Gee, I sure would have liked to be on the trip. I want to taste some of your spaghetti and meat balls later on."

John asked me, "Is "Tiny" mad at me?" I said, "No, he has a hangover. He was as drunk as a skunk last night." About half an hour later "Tiny" joined us. We were throwing the bull around until Carol said, "How about making some meatballs for Spencer Tracy?"

They had all the canned goods. I bought some fresh hamburger and pot roast. They had a nice iron pot. It was beautiful to cook spaghetti sauce in. I let it simmer while we were swimming and then I served it. Spencer Tracy said, "I wish I'd been on that trip. Anytime you're down in Southern California, come on and look me up!"

That night when we were leaving John told us that he had rented a little log cabin house on Eardley Street in Pacific Grove to do his writing. He said, "What's wrong with you guys? Why don't you come up and see me sometime?"

One day a couple of weeks later when we had nothing to do, we went over to see him. Just as we got in the place, Carol came up and said to us, "You're just in time to celebrate. I'm going to Hawaii to have the little bastard."

We said, "What?" because we didn't know what she meant. So she brought in a gallon of wine and we all sat on the floor. They always liked to do that. We were on our second glass of wine when we heard a car horn blow. John went out and when he came back he said, "Do you guys mind leaving? I've got a little business to attend to here." Outside we saw a young blonde woman in a car, crying.

Later we figured it out. The young blonde was Gwen Conger who claimed to be pregnant. Evidently they were going over there so she could have the baby and then Carol and John would pretend it was theirs. But instead John and Carol had an argument and got divorced. Later he married Gwen.

Another time we met John for a drink. He was having a love affair with the movie star, Paulette Goddard. He kept saying to us, "I don't know what she sees in me. I can't give her money or movie parts and I'm not handsome. She's got plenty of good looks, better looking men than me, plenty of money and all the good parts she wants in the movies."

"Maybe it's because you're a stud, John," "Tiny" told him. "Hell, can't you read between the lines?"

Afterwards we heard that he hung a pair of her black lace panties in his den. He put a little sign under them that read "Won in the field of battle—and not a very big one at that."

After the war started we began to lose touch. Carol wrote to me a few times, but I couldn't get John's address. I asked Peter Ferrante and Toby Street for it but they never gave it to me. Then I was stationed in Rome at the same time that John was there. I had read about him in "Stars and Stripes." Finally, I got a five day pass to Rome but I didn't have his address.

When I got back there was a letter from Steinbeck waiting for me. It was postmarked Italy. This is what it said: "If you're ever in Rome, if I'm not there, look up Governor Palatti, the Allied Commander and the ex-Governor of New York. Look him up and he'll fix you up with a couple of redheads." A buddy of mine said, "I'd like to have that letter," so I gave it to him.

Once we met Carol in a bar in Monterey and I bought her a drink. Then "Tiny" bought her a drink. It was June and there hadn't been any fishing, so "Tiny" says, "Carol, aren't you going to buy me a drink?" She told us she didn't have any money so "Tiny" says, "Well, write a check." She told him she didn't like to write checks. "The hell with you", he said. "Sparky", let's get outta here."

We went down to another bar called Jesenetta's Bar. We met two girls and were drinking with them when we heard a voice say, "Are "Sparky" and "Tiny" in there?" About ten minutes later she came in and said, "I cashed a check. I'll buy you guys a drink." "Tiny" answered, "Now we're with two girls, so you'll have to buy them a drink, too."

During the war Carol was a volunteer at the hospital in Fort Ord. She was sort of a nurse's aide when my wife went there to have her son. She thought Carol was odd and had heard strange stories about her.

After the war I got about five or six letters from John. He always said he would be coming back to see me soon, but he never did. I was bartending at the Dew Drop Inn in those days. I'd read them to the young soldiers. If they asked me for them, I'd give them the letters. What the hell! They might never come back. Sometimes now I wish I still had them.

Once I loaned out my copy of Sea of Cortez and it was never returned. I wrote to John and he sent me another autographed one. When he came back from Doc's funeral, I was out of town. We just kept missing each other.

But then, maybe John had changed. I saw those pictures of him in the Salinas Library with his third wife, Elaine. My God—suits, ties, overcoats and even a tuxedo when he got the Nobel Prize. I had never seen him in anything but levis and an old seaman's cap. So that's probably why I never saw him again. He was a completely different kind of guy.

WHERE HAVE ALL THE CREW GONE?

"Tiny" was the first one to go. He had an enlarged heart. I guess all that carousing did him in. When I got back from overseas in 1945 I thought he looked awfully thin. Two months later he died. He had been in the service but had received a medical discharge.

He had married a Mexican woman and he had a boy. I met his wife later and the boy looked just like "Tiny." They're back East somewhere and I haven't seen them since.

At the time of his death he was going around with a girl, so I tried to take care of her for about six months after his death. I paid her rent and took her out. She was in the rackets and on dope, so that was no life for me. Finally, I told her, "You go your way and I'll go mine."

It still seems to me that "Tiny" should be here. He died too young. I miss him.

When "Doc" got killed, I was in Mexico fishing for tuna. We used to go for fifty or sixty days at a time. When I got back it was all over. The papers were gone and I only heard what people told me. The Del Monte Express always went through at about three a.m. in the morning. It hit Doc's car. He might have been drunk or fallen asleep at the wheel, or maybe the car stalled. Nobody knows what happened.

John came back for the funeral, and George Robinson, a mutual friend, told me that he and John went over to the lab after the funeral. John wanted to burn all the personal papers that "Doc" had in his safe. Again, nobody knows why.

John died in New York in 1968. They had a big funeral back there for him, but they brought his ashes back here. I heard that his family had a private service for him back here and scattered his ashes over Point Lobos. That was always one of his favorite places.

Sparky looks at the newly unveiled bust of Steinbeck in the middle of Cannery Row. Courtesy of the Enea family.

Carol had a brief marriage after her divorce from John. Then she married Bill Brown whose family owned the Palace Hotel in San Francisco. They lived in Carmel. I knew Bill from high school. Over the years I used to see Carol in all the bars along the Row but in the last five years before her death, I only saw her to say, "Hello."

"Tex" married the girl he was engaged to when we left for the Sea of Cortez. They had four kids—two boys and two girls. He moved to San Pedro and retired to Lake Havazu in Arizona. We kept track of each other because he has relatives in Monterey. Once he called me to talk, but I could hardly understand him because he had part of his tongue removed for cancer. He died in 1990.

After the war I continued to be a fisherman, and for many years I would fish for five or six months every year up in Alaska. I always liked the life of a fisherman and I always wanted to go back to the Sea of Cortez. Mainly I wanted to buy a boat of my own or even go down there with somebody else and stay there for a couple of months. When I think of how I never went back, I could kick my behind.

When my fishing career ended, I became a bartender at Johnny's Dew Drop Inn. Over the years it gradually turned into a gay bar. I heard lots of good stories over the years in that bar and I always hoped I could tell them to John so that he could write them.

For the last few years I've spent a lot of time caddying. Usually every year I worked at the annual Crosby Golf Tournament where I caddied for a lot of famous people like Alan Shepherd and Joe Montana. Since I turned eighty I just do occasional caddy work.

Captain Tony Berry continued his fishing career until his retirement. He is married to my sister, Rose, and they live in Monterey. Occasionally we get together and talk about our trip to the Sea of Cortez. Sometimes we argue over certain points that Steinbeck put in the book. Sometimes I tell him things that he didn't know at the time. Either way, we always laugh a lot!

AFTERWORD

Horace Sparky Enea, aged 80, comes from a long line of Sicilian fisherman. He has lived his life in Monterey California, the city long associated with the famous author John Steinbeck. At an early age he was nicknamed Sparky after Sparkplug, a character in the old Barney Google comic strip.

Sparky attended Monterey schools and graduated from Monterey High School. During his school days he was very active in sports, especially boxing and football. During World War II he served in the Navy in Italy. After his stint in the Navy he married Mary Correa, a cannery worker. Mary had a son by a previous marriage but the Eneas have no children.

For most of his working life Sparky has been a fisherman like his father before him. His father owned a fishing boat and was part of the sardine fleet that originally attracted old world fisherman to life in America. Eventually the elder Enea invested in a cannery of his own, but he lost it and his boat when the sardines suddenly disappeared from the Monterey Bay.

In 1939 Sparky was catapulted to local fame when he accompanied John Steinbeck and Edward Ricketts on the now famous trip to the Sea of Cortez. He was hired as a deck hand and turned out to be cook as well. His recollections of the incidents and people along on that trip are a valuable insight into literary history. His memoir is not a sophisticated record but an anecdotal one, full of natural bias and fun. At the time of this writing, Sparky remains one of the few authentic Steinbeck characters left on Cannery Row.

After his career as a fishermen ended, Sparky became a well-liked bartender in Monterey. In recent years he has enjoyed caddying for famous personalities at local golf classics.

Sparky Enea passed away in January 1994. His friends and family miss him.

WITH THE STEINBECK/ RICKETTS EXPEDITION

In 1940, John Steinbeck, newly famous from the publication of *GRAPES OF WRATH* spent the spring collecting marine specimens with Edward Ricketts and five others board a 76 foot purse seiner called the Western Flyer. Their destination was the Sea of Cortez. Also along on this famous expedition were Steinbeck's wife, Carol, Captain Tony Berry, Tex, the engineer, and two crew members Sparky Enea and "Tiny" Colleto, all later immortalized in Steinbeck's book *SEA OF CORTEZ: A LEISURELY JOURNAL OF TRAVEL AND RESEARCH.*

Here is Sparky Enea's humorous and savvy version of those remarkable days adrift off Baja, California. He tells true tales of Cannery Row, "Doc" Ricketts and the Western Flyer's rambunctious Baja adventure. Here is the real story of the enduring legend, John Steinbeck, and Sparky's personal Log from the Sea of Cortez, recounting those wild and heady days. Follow Sparky to La Paz, and Guaymas, and through days and nights of madcap marine specimen collecting as he and the rest of the crew of the Western Flyer make literary history.

Audry Lynch was born and raised in Cambridge, Massachusetts. Her lifelong interest in John Steinbeck has led her in many directions. To date her most exciting Steinbeck discoveries have emerged from her remarkable friendship with Sparky Enea. After countless hours of interviews Dr. Lynch has helped Sparky to reconstruct the ambience of the Steinbeck/Ricketts Expedition to the Sea of Cortez, with all its fascinating color and detail. Here are hitherto unknown stories of that historic trip, combined with some recently discovered and previously unpublished pictures. This book is sure to add to the legend of one of America's foremost writers.

INDEX